HOW LEAVES CHANGE

HOW LEAVES CHANGE

by Sylvia A. Johnson

Photographs by Yuko Sato

A Lerner Natural Science Book

Lerner Publications Company ▪ Minneapolis

Syliva A. Johnson, Series Editor

Translation of original text by Phyllis Hyland Larson

The publisher wishes to thank Roberta Sladky, Department of Botany, University of Minnesota, for her assistance in the preparation of this book.

Additional photographs by: pp. 10 (left), 17, Hiroo Koike; pp. 11 (lower right), 21, Shabo Hani; p. 43, S.A. Johnson. Drawing by Joji Umemura.

The glossary on page 46 gives definitions and pronunciations of words shown in **bold type** in the text.

This book is available in two editions:
Library binding by Lerner Publications Company
Soft Cover by First Avenue Editions
241 First Avenue North
Minneapolis, Minnesota 55401

LIBRARY OF CONGRESS CATALOGING-IN-PUBLICATION DATA

Johnson, Sylvia A.
How leaves change.

(A Lerner natural science book)
Adaptation of: Kōyō no fushigi/Satō Yūkō.
Includes index.
Summary: Describes the structure and purpose of leaves, the ways in which they change as part of the natural cycle of the seasons, and the process that creates their autumn colors.
1. Leaves — Juvenile literature. 2. Leaves — Development — Juvenile literature. 3. Fall foliage — Juvenile literature. [1. Leaves. 2. Fall foliage. 3. Seasons]
I. Satō, Yūkō, 1928-   . ill. II. Satō, Yūkō, 1928-
Kōyō no fushigi. III. Title. IV. Series.
QK649.J64 1986   581.1'0427   86-10545
ISBN: 0-8225-1483-4 (lib. bdg.)

International Standard Book Number: 0-8225-1483-4 (lib. bdg.)
International Standard Book Number: 0-8225-9513-3 (pbk.)
Library of Congress Catalog Number: 86-10545

8   9   10   96   95   94   93   92   91

People who live in parts of the world where there are four different seasons enjoy many natural wonders throughout the year. Winter's crisp cold and glittering snow are followed by the balmy air and fresh green of spring. Summer brings increased warmth and a deep, lush green, as trees and other plants thrive in the heat of the summer sun.

For many people, however, autumn is the season that gives the greatest pleasure. The sun's light cools to a gentle glow, and the green leaves of summer undergo a remarkable change. They gradually take on the colors of a bonfire—pale yellows, deep golds, and reds ranging from orange to scarlet to rust.

What causes leaves to be transformed in such an amazing way year after year? This book will explain the process that creates autumn colors and describe the complex natural cycle of which they are a part.

In the autumn, the leaves of many deciduous trees change color (opposite) before falling from the branches. Evergreen trees like the red pine (left) and the cedar (right) keep their green leaves all year round.

LEAVES THROUGHOUT THE YEAR

If you live in a tropical part of the world, you have probably never seen the riot of colors that people in many temperate areas enjoy every autumn. You have also missed this spectacle if your home is in a northern region where most of the trees are pines and firs.

Such trees, as well as those that grow in the tropics, are **evergreens** whose leaves do not change color and fall every year. Evergreen trees have their own cycles of change and growth, but these patterns are not clearly reflected in their leaves. It is only the **deciduous trees** of temperate regions that reveal their inner lives in the color and condition of their leaves.

New leaves that appear in the spring are a soft, fresh green.

SPRING: NEW LEAVES UNFOLD

The delicate, fresh green that brightens a spring landscape is the green of new leaves that have appeared on deciduous trees and other plants. Tree branches that have been bare throughout the winter are now studded with opening **buds.** These small bundles of tiny folded leaves and twigs have actually been on the trees all winter, perhaps hidden under a coat of snow. As the spring days become longer and the warmth of the sun increases, the buds begin their development.

The timing of this natural process is so precise that all the similar kinds of trees in one limited geographical area usually open their leaves on exactly the same day. This amazing event does not occur on the same day every spring since weather conditions vary from year to year. Variations in a tree's environment—for example, whether it grows on a hill or in a hollow—can also affect the timing. In general, however, the leaf buds of each kind of tree burst open within hours of each other, responding to a message communicated by the environment.

As young leaves develop, their green color becomes deeper and darker.

Apple trees bear beautiful flowers in shades of pink and white (left). The pink "petals" of this flowering dogwood (right) are actually special leaves known as bracts.

The opening of some tree buds reveals flowers as well as leaves, while other buds contain only flowers. On many deciduous trees such as maples and elms, the flower buds open before the leaves have appeared. Other trees produce flowers and leaves at the same time.

Like the flowers of all green plants, tree flowers contain the male and female reproductive parts that will produce seeds from which new trees grow. Unlike the flowers of soft-stemmed plants such as roses and lilies, most tree flowers are small and inconspicuous. Some fruit trees and ornamental trees like crabapples, however, do have colorful, fragrant flowers.

The flowering dogwood tree (shown above) bears leaves that masquerade as flowers. The beautiful white or pink "petals" seen on dogwood trees in the spring are actually special leaves known as **bracts**. A dogwood's real flowers are clustered within the circle of bracts.

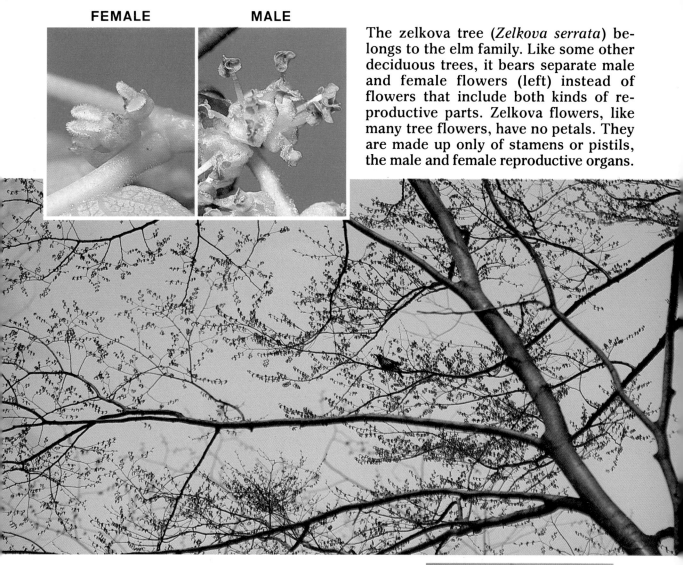

FEMALE　　**MALE**

The zelkova tree (*Zelkova serrata*) belongs to the elm family. Like some other deciduous trees, it bears separate male and female flowers (left) instead of flowers that include both kinds of reproductive parts. Zelkova flowers, like many tree flowers, have no petals. They are made up only of stamens or pistils, the male and female reproductive organs.

The delicate flower of the Japanese maple (right) includes both the female pistil and male stamens. These reproductive organs are surrounded by small petals.

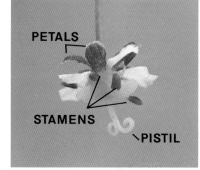

PETALS

STAMENS

PISTIL

Young leaves of a ginkgo tree (left) and a persimmon tree (right)

THE ROLE OF THE LEAF

Flowers are important in the life of a tree because they make reproduction possible. Leaves play an even more essential role: they supply the nourishment that allows a tree to carry on all its life processes. Soon after they unfold in the spring, the new young leaves take on the job of making food.

The way in which the leaves of trees and other plants produce food has amazed and puzzled scientists for many years. Today, much is understood about this complicated method, known as **photosynthesis**.

The word *photosynthesis* means "putting together with light," and that is exactly what leaves do. They produce food by using the energy of the sun to combine raw materials drawn

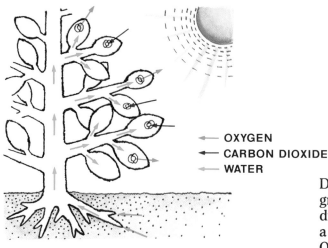

OXYGEN
CARBON DIOXIDE
WATER

During photosynthesis, a green plant combines carbon dioxide and water to produce a sugar known as glucose. Oxygen is a byproduct of this process.

from the soil and the air. The basic ingredients that a plant needs for photosynthesis are carbon dioxide, water, and, of course, sunlight.

Carbon dioxide is a gas given off by living things during the process of respiration. It is taken into a plant leaf through tiny openings or pores on its surface called **stomata**. The other essential ingredient, water, is drawn up from the soil by the roots and carried to the leaf through the tubes or veins of the tree's **vascular system**.

When these raw materials enter a leaf that is exposed to sunlight, photosynthesis takes place. The food-making process occurs in special cells that fill the center of a leaf, between the two outer layers of **epidermis**. The cells in this area, known as the **mesophyll**, contain tiny bodies called **chloroplasts**. Within the chloroplasts are molecules of the green pigment **chlorophyll**. It is this material that not only gives leaves their green color but also makes photosynthesis possible.

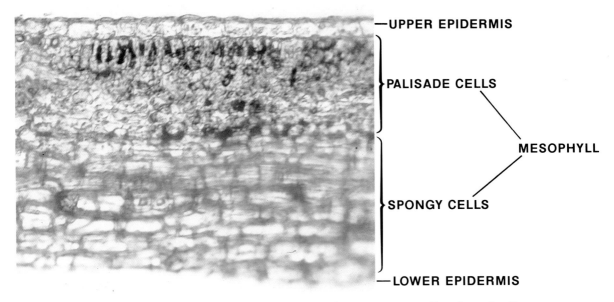

—UPPER EPIDERMIS

PALISADE CELLS

SPONGY CELLS

MESOPHYLL

LOWER EPIDERMIS

This cross-section photograph shows the structure of a plant leaf. The mesophyll, where photosynthesis takes place, is made up of two kinds of cells: long, narrow palisade cells, located below the upper epidermis, and irregularly shaped spongy cells, which are surrounded by air spaces. These cells, especially the palisade cells, contain many chloroplasts that are filled with the green food-making pigment chlorophyll.

By absorbing sunlight, chlorophyll produces the energy that breaks down and then combines molecules of water and carbon dioxide. The results of this synthesis are two new substances—oxygen and a form of sugar known as **glucose**.

Glucose is the basic food used by a plant in growing, reproducing, and carrying on all of its life processes. The plant also uses some oxygen, but most of this gas is released through the stomata into the atmosphere. Here it supplies the essential element for the respiration of all forms of animal life, including human beings.

REMOVING CHLOROPHYLL FROM A PLANT LEAF

Chlorophyll is a pigment, or coloring agent, that can actually be extracted from a leaf. In the experiment shown here, a leaf from a zelkova tree was first soaked in boiling water and then placed in a beaker of alcohol, which was set in a container of warm water for about an hour. During this time, the alcohol solution gradually turned green as the chlorophyll was drawn out of the leaf (right).

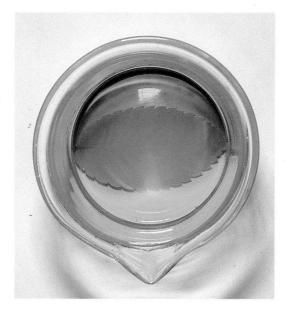

Before the experiment, the leaf is a bright green, its cells filled with chlorophyll (above).

After the experiment, the leaf is completely white, its chlorophyll now contained in the alcohol solution (right).

The hot sun of midsummer shines through the fully developed leaves of a zelkova tree.

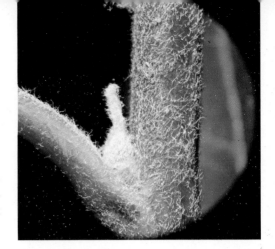

A bud begins to develop on an apple tree. It is covered with a protective coat of hairy fibers.

SUMMER LEAVES: FOOD FOR GROWTH

Summer is the season when the leaves of deciduous trees work the hardest. Using the energy of the bright summer sun, they spend the daylight hours producing food by means of photosynthesis. The glucose manufactured in the leaves is sent to all parts of the tree through the tubes of the vascular system and used in the production of new cells.

During the day, leaves usually manufacture more glucose than the tree can use. The excess glucose is transformed into another carbohydrate, starch, and stored in the chloroplasts. During the dark hours of the night, part of the stored starch is turned back into glucose and used to fuel the activities of the tree's cells.

Some of the food produced by the leaves is used to prepare for a future season of growth. During the summer, many trees begin to form buds enclosing new leaves, twigs, and flowers. The buds will live through the coming winter and then open in the spring.

17

Small sacs at the ends of zelkova leaves (left) are made by a kind of beetle that goes through its pupal stage (above left) hidden inside. Adult beetles (above right) and other insects feed on tree leaves, leaving them tattered and full of holes (opposite).

Leaves often nourish other living things as well as the tree on which they grow. Birds and insects feed on the leaves of many trees. Some insects like certain kinds of beetles go through their whole life cycle among the leaves. The adult insects eat the leaves and lay their eggs on them. The larvae that hatch from the eggs also feed on the tender green leaf tissue. In the pupal stage, the insects make protective cases on the leaves and finish their development inside.

The insects that live in and around a tree use the energy created through photosynthesis when they eat the tree's leaves or suck its sap. Birds and other animals that in turn eat the insects also get their nourishment from the food-making ability of green plants.

18

The fruit of an apple tree encloses and protects the seeds from which new trees grow.

During the spring and summer growing period, some of the food energy manufactured by the leaves is used in the production of seeds. Like all plant seeds, the seeds of trees are created through sexual reproduction. The sperm cells produced by the male parts of a tree's flowers are united with the female egg cells, usually with the help of pollinating insects or the wind. The fertilized eggs develop into seeds that contain all the parts necessary to produce new plants.

Tree seeds, like all plant seeds, are enclosed and protected in **fruits** that develop from the female parts of the flowers. The fruits of apple and peach trees are soft and juicy, but many trees produce hard, dry fruits. Trees like walnuts and pecans have the kind of fruit known as a nut.

20

Maple trees have dry and papery fruits with little "wings" that allow them to float on the wind.

When the zelkova tree has finished the job of producing seeds, it begins to prepare for winter. The inset photograph shows the tiny green fruit of the zelkova.

AUTUMN: THE GREAT CHANGE BEGINS

The seeds of different kinds of trees develop at different times during the late spring and summer. When autumn arrives, deciduous trees have finished the job of seed-making. They are now entering a new stage in their lives, and their leaves signal the great change.

In autumn, deciduous trees prepare for the coming winter, which will be a season of inactivity and rest. Like most green plants, trees cannot continue to function during the winter as they do in other times of the year. Their food-making processes depend on sunlight and moisture, which are in short supply during the winter months.

Woody plants like trees and shrubs maintain minimum cell activity during this period by using the food energy stored in their tissues. Soft-stemmed **perennial** plants like some garden flowers keep only their roots or bulbs alive, dying off above the ground. **Annual** plants live for just one growing season and survive only in the seeds that they produce.

As the chlorophyll in the cells of this maple leaf disappears, other pigments are revealed.

As deciduous trees approach the end of their food-making period each autumn, the amount of chlorophyll in their leaves begins to decrease. Since photosynthesis will soon come to an end, the green pigment no longer has a role to play in the tree's life. This gradual disappearance of chlorophyll explains why leaves lose their green color, but what causes the green to be replaced with yellows, oranges, and reds?

The answer to this question is complicated, but part of the solution lies in the fact that some of the other colors are already present in the leaf. During spring and summer, they are hidden by the intense green of the chlorophyll. As the chlorophyll fades away, the leaf's other pigments are revealed.

25

Opposite: Carotene and xanthophyll pigments are responsible for the beautiful orange and gold colors of these leaves.

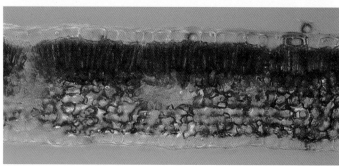

Left: These cross-section photographs show the change in a leaf's palisade cells as the green chlorophyll gives way to the orange carotene pigments.

Within the chloroplasts of a leaf's cells are molecules of two other kinds of pigments in addition to chlorophyll. These two groups of coloring agents, known as **carotenes** and **xanthophylls**, produce the vibrant yellow, gold, and orange colors of autumn leaves.

The yellow and orange pigments found in leaves are common in the plant world. Carotene pigments are responsible for the yellow of bananas and the golden-orange of carrots, sweet potatoes, and pumpkins. Yellow and orange flowers get their hues from the carotene or xanthophyll pigments contained in small bodies called **chromoplasts**, found within the cells of their petals. (*Chloroplast* is the special name for a chromoplast that contains chlorophyll.)

The yellows and oranges of an autumn landscape are created when the hidden pigments in leaves are revealed, but the beautiful red colors come from another source. The pigments responsible for the scarlets, rusts, and purples of autumn appear only at this time of year. They are not already present in the leaves as the other pigments are.

Maple trees often develop deep red leaves in the autumn. The intense color is produced by anthocyanin pigments.

Anthocyanin pigments are the ones that paint autumn leaves in shades of red. Like the yellow and orange pigments, this group is also found in many growing things, including bright-red radishes, deep-red beets, and purple-blue flowers like morning glories and hyacinths.

These beautiful red pigments develop in autumn leaves as a result of the shutdown of a tree's food-processing system. At the same time that the production of chlorophyll ceases, the flow of water and glucose between the leaves and the tree comes to an end. At the point where a leaf stalk joins a branch, a layer of special cells develops. This layer, called the **abscission** or **separation layer**, gradually blocks the tiny veins that carry material between the leaf and the rest of the tree.

Opposite: A zelkova tree puts on its autumn colors.

When a leaf loses its connection to the tree's vascular system, some glucose usually remains within its mesophyll cells. It is this trapped glucose that develops into the red anthocyanin pigments. Bright sunlight and cool nighttime temperatures are required in order for this chemical change to take place. Frost, on the other hand, kills leaves. In years where there is an early frost, leaves are likely to become brown and dry rather than vividly colored.

This experiment demonstrates the way in which the development of red pigments in leaves depends on sunlight. A Boston ivy leaf was partly covered by a piece of tape (1), which was left in place during the period of color change in the autumn (2). The part of the leaf exposed to the sun turned a deep red, while the part hidden under the tape became yellow (2 and 3). As we have seen, the pigments responsible for yellow colors are revealed when the chlorophyll disappears, while red pigments develop only in the presence of sunlight.

A GALLERY OF AUTUMN COLORS

Deciduous trees and other woody plants produce a great variety of colors during the brief weeks of autumn. The colors of the leaves on a particular tree depend on many factors, including the type of tree and its inherited characteristics, as well as weather conditions in that year.

In general, trees like maples (opposite, upper left) that produce large amounts of glucose tend to have red leaves because the red anthocyanin pigments develop from this sugar. If such trees do not receive adequate sunlight, their leaves will show only the yellow and orange of the other two groups of pigments. When red pigments do develop in leaves, they usually conceal the lighter colors.

32

Trees are not the only plants that display vivid colors in the autumn. All green plants contain carotene and xanthophyll pigments, which are revealed when the chlorophyll begins to disappear from their leaves. Many grasses display beautiful shades of yellow and gold, while other plants like poison ivy develop the red anthocyanin pigments. This vine, like its relatives in the sumac family, is known for the vibrant red of its autumn leaves.

This colorful Asian member of the sumac family is a close relative of the North American poison ivy.

At the end of summer, the pokeweed plant bears clusters of
small fruits (right). Its leaves are
still green and filled with chlorophyll (below).

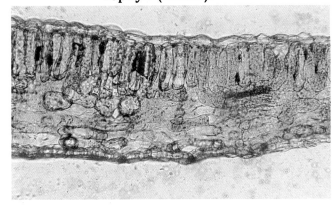

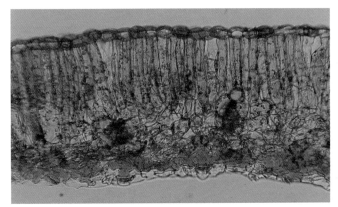

During the months of autumn,
the pokeweed's seeds are scat-
tered (right), and its leaves begin
to develop red pigments (above).

This cross-section photograph shows winter buds on a maple tree.

WINTER BUDS

The colors of autumn leaves are bright and vivid, but they are signs of decay and an end to life. Leaves exhibit these brilliant colors only briefly before they wither and fall from the trees. Although the leaves die in autumn, other parts of the tree are bursting with life.

The leaf and flower buds that began to grow during the summer have now completed their development and are ready to face the coming winter. These **winter buds** are made up of tiny folded leaves and other plant parts. They are covered by tough **bud scales** that will keep in the moisture necessary for survival during the harsh months ahead.

In most trees, winter buds grow in the **leaf axils**, just above the points where the stalks, or **petioles**, of the old leaves are connected to the tree's branches. When the leaves fall from the tree, the buds will remain, their precious contents preserved and protected until the following spring.

36

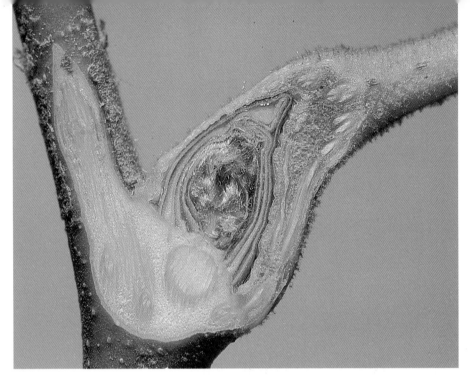

Plane trees, like other members of the sycamore family, have winter buds that grow in an unusual location. They develop inside the hollow, enlarged ends of the leaf stalks (above). When the leaves fall in the autumn, the large cone-shaped buds are revealed (below).

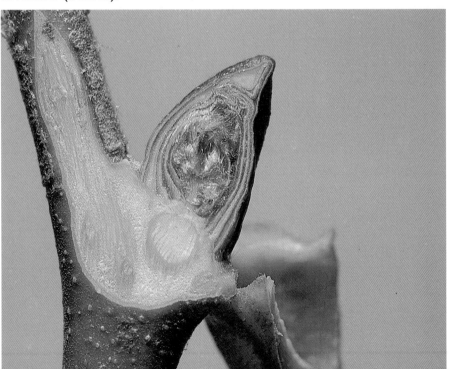

AUTUMN MEANS FALL

In some English-speaking countries, the season of autumn is also called *fall* because the falling of tree leaves seems to symbolize this beautiful but rather sad time of year. A fascinating natural process known as **abscission** causes leaves to drift down from their branches and carpet the ground.

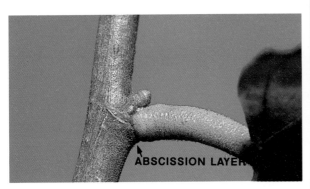

ABSCISSION LAYER

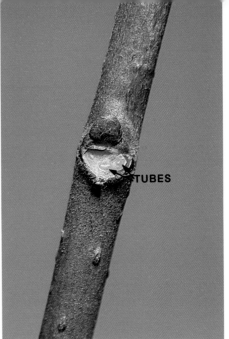

TUBES

The breakdown of cells in the abscission layer (above) causes a leaf to fall from the tree. At the point where the leaf was attached, you can see the ends of the tiny tubes that are part of the tree's vascular system (right).

The abscission layer of cells, which earlier formed at the base of the leaf stalk and cut the leaf off from the tree's vascular system, is also responsible for its fall. After the shutdown of food production is completed, the cells in the abscission layer begin to dissolve. Soon the leaf is attached to its branch only by the bundles of tiny vascular tubes that once carried water and nutrients between the leaf and the rest of the tree.

As the tree is battered by the gusty winds and pelting rains of autumn, these frail connections eventually let go. The leaf, now dead and dry, falls to the ground. To protect the tissue of the tree branch, a layer of corky material develops over the spot where the leaf was attached. Within this **leaf scar**, you can usually see clusters of tiny dots. These are the remains of the tubes that once ran from the branch into the leaf stalk.

After leaves fall to the ground, their lives are over, but they still have a role to play in the natural environment. The litter of decaying leaves on the forest floor provides shelter and food for many living creatures, including the larvae of beetles (left) and adult insects such as springtails (upper right) and lice (lower right).

Mushrooms and other fungi grow on the dead leaves, taking their nourishment from the nutrients originally produced by photosynthesis. As the tree leaves decay and disintegrate (opposite), they enrich the soil for the growth of other plants.

Left: The bare branches of this zelkova tree wear a blanket of snow. *Right:* The camphor tree is a broadleaf tree that keeps its leaves in winter.

GREEN LEAVES THROUGHOUT THE WINTER

After its leaves fall, a deciduous tree stands bare, its branches exposed to the cold and snow of winter. Evergreen trees keep their green leaves all winter long, although they do not photosynthesize during the cold, sunless months.

The most common kinds of evergreens in North America are pines, firs, spruces, and other trees with long, needle-shaped leaves. These thin, narrow leaves are more resistant to cold and lack of moisture than the flat, broad leaves of most deciduous trees. A few kinds of evergreen trees that grow in temperate climates do have broad leaves but with tough, leathery surfaces. With these kinds of leaves, trees like

Forests of needleleaf evergreen trees are often found on the slopes of mountains.

holly and myrtle can withstand winter weather, although not the extreme conditions under which needleleaf trees survive.

Evergreen trees do not shed all their leaves in autumn like deciduous trees, but they do lose old leaves from time to time and replace them with new ones. This change takes place throughout the year so that an evergreen is never completely leafless. Evergreens in tropical areas not only have leaves all year round but also continue to grow and produce food.

Left: Some oak trees keep their dead leaves throughout the winter. *Above:* Coated with ice, winter buds of a zelkova tree await the coming of spring.

THE LONG WAIT FOR SPRING

For deciduous trees, winter is a season of **dormancy**, or rest. Food production ceases, and the tree lives on its stored supply of starch. Tossed by gales and pelted by ice and snow, it stands firm, awaiting the coming of spring.

Many deciduous trees need the period of winter dormancy in order to continue their natural functioning during the rest of the year. Their winter buds will not open in the spring unless the trees have experienced a period of low temperatures. Fruit trees like the apple, peach, and cherry require a long winter rest. Many kinds of peach trees, for example, must go through 600 to 900 hours of temperatures below 45 degrees Fahrenheit (about 8 degrees Celsius) before they will produce leaves and flowers in the spring.

After resting through the winter, a deciduous tree will burst forth in fresh green leaves, beginning the cycle of change that will once again end in a blaze of autumn colors.

A grove of zelkova trees on a winter night. In a few months' time, their branches will be covered by new green leaves.

GLOSSARY

abscission (ab-SIZH-uhn)—the natural process that separates leaves and other plant parts from the plants on which they grow

annual—living for only one growing season

anthocyanin (an-thuh-SI-ih-nuhn) pigments—pigments that create the red colors in plant leaves

bud scales—scale-like coverings that protect winter buds

buds—the parts of a plant that will develop into new leaves and flowers

carotenes (KAR-uh-teens)—pigments in plants and other living things that produce orange and yellow colors

chlorophyll (KLOR-uh-fil)—the green pigment in plant leaves that makes photosynthesis possible

chloroplasts (KLOR-uh-plasts)—tiny bodies in the cells of a plant leaf that contain chlorophyll and other pigments

chromoplasts (KRO-muh-plasts)—tiny bodies in plant cells that contain pigments

deciduous (dih-SIJ-u-ous) trees—trees that shed their leaves in the autumn

dormancy (DOR-muhn-see)—a state of rest or inactivity

epidermis (ep-ih-DER-muhs)—the thin outer layer of a plant leaf

evergreens—trees that keep their leaves all year round

fruits—the parts of a plant that enclose and protect the seeds

46

glucose (GLU-kose)—a kind of sugar produced by plants during photosynthesis

leaf axils (AK-sils)—the angles formed between leaf stalks and the branches to which they are attached

leaf scar—an area of corky material that forms over the spot where a fallen leaf was attached to a branch

mesophyll (MEZ-ih-fil)—the middle layer of a plant leaf, where photosynthesis takes place

perennial (puh-REN-ee-uhl)—surviving for more than one season

petioles (PET-ee-oles)—the stalks of leaves

photosynthesis (fot-uh-SIN-thih-sis)—the process by which green plants use the energy of the sun to make food

separation layer—a layer of specialized cells at the base of a leaf or other plant part. The breakdown of these cells causes leaves, flowers, and fruits to fall.

stomata (STO-muh-tuh)—the tiny pores or openings in a plant leaf. The singular form of the word is **stoma**.

vacuoles (VAK-yu-woles)—fluid-filled spaces in plant cells where anthocyanin pigments form

vascular (VAS-kyu-luhr) system—the system of small tubes or veins that carry water and nutrients to all parts of a plant

winter buds—buds that form during the growing season and live through the winter, opening the following spring

xanthophylls (ZAN-thih-fils)—pigments in plants and other living things that produce yellow and orange colors

INDEX